UNRAVELING THE MYSTERIES OF VOCAL TECHNIQUE

UNRAVELING THE MYSTERIES OF VOCAL TECHNIQUE

CONCEPTIONS & MisCONCEPTIONS
about Singing

Ruth Manahan and Marise Petry

Copyright © 2011 by Ruth Manahan and Marise Petry.

Library of Congress Control Number:		2011909867
ISBN:	Hardcover	978-1-4628-8857-3
	Softcover	978-1-4628-8856-6
	Ebook	978-1-4628-8858-0

All rights reserved. No part of this book may be reproduced or transmitted in any form or by any means, electronic or mechanical, including photocopying, recording, or by any information storage and retrieval system, without permission in writing from the copyright owner.

This book was printed in the United States of America.

To order additional copies of this book, contact:
Xlibris Corporation
1-888-795-4274
www.Xlibris.com
Orders@Xlibris.com

CONTENTS

Forward 11

CHAPTER ONE
The Body

Lesson One: Posture 17
Lesson Two: Posture And Tension Related To Posture 21
Lesson Three: Posture With Emphasis On Relaxation Of Muscles 24
Lesson Four: Posture Of The Voice 28

CHAPTER TWO
Breathing

Lesson One: Locate The Breath 35
Lesson Two-A: Inhale 38
Lesson Two-B: Inhale (continued) 41
Lesson Three: Exhale and Sing 44
Lesson Four: Breath Control And Support 47
Lesson Five: Breath Control And Energy 50

CHAPTER THREE
The Tongue

Lesson One: "Taming The Shrewish Tongue"
    The Tongue As A Hinderance To Vocal Production 57
Lesson Two: "The Martyr Tongue" 61

CHAPTER FOUR
Tone Quality

Lesson One-A: Vocal Placement—The Floating Tone 67
Lesson One-B: Vocal Placement—The Floating Tone continued 69
Lesson Two: The Effect Of Speech Patterns
   [This comes from a conversation with Eileen Davis] 72
Lesson Three: What Else Can Affect Tone Quality? 74
Lesson Four: The Hard And Soft Palates 76
Lesson Five: The "Cover" 7

CHAPTER FIVE
Legato and Staccato Articulation

Lesson One: Legato 85
Lesson Two: Staccato 87

CHAPTER SIX
Diction (in English)

Lesson One: The Lips, Vowels, Diphthongs 93
Lesson Two: Consonants 95
Lesson Three: Modifying The Vowel 97
Lesson Four: The Rules Of Diction 99

CHAPTER SEVEN
Registers and classifying the voice, working with children and the male voice

Lesson One: Chest, Middle, Passáge, Head, Whistle, FalsettO 105
Lesson Two: Bridging The Gap Between Registers 108
Lesson Three: If And When A Voice Can/Should Be Classified
   Teaching Children And Working With The Male Voice 111

CHAPTER EIGHT
The Performance

Lesson One: Performance Readiness 119
Lesson Two: The Physical Experience... 121
Lesson Three: Food, Drink And Other Things
    That May Help Or Hurt The Voice 123

CHAPTER NINE
Trilling

Lesson One: The Trill 129

APPENDIX

Notes From Lessons With Eleanor Steber... 133
Upon Losing 100 Pounds And Its Effect On My Singing...................... 139
Vocal Exercises: what they emphasize and how to use them 140

DEDICATION

To Eleanor Steber not only my mentor,
but my friend and the inspiration for this book.
Ruth

To my teacher, mentor, colleague and dear friend, Ruth Manahan. Thank you for all you've taught me.

To my husband, John for his support and encouragement over the many years that the development of this book has taken. You are my anchor.

Marise

To Eileen Davis for her opinions and help in this manuscript.

To Paula Trybus and Sue Wiechart-White for your input.

To our vocal students for letting us experiment and offering your insights as to how you might understand vocal concepts better.
Ruth and Marise

FORWARD

Who We Are

- By way of introduction, we include here our credentials.
- Ruth Manahan
    - Lifelong singer. Ruth remembers singing as far back as she can remember, especially beginning in the 3rd grade.
    - Due to incorrect training, she lost her voice. That is what led her to audition in 1962 with Eleanor Steber who was teaching at the Cleveland Institute of Music at the time. Her studies with Eleanor included 5 years of vocal pedagogy
    - She has studied at Stoney Brook College in New York and at Temple University. While in New York, she studied several summers with Mr. Buchwalter, the coach at the Metropolitan of Opera. She has had several lessons in New York with Marni Nixon. In Ohio, she has also studied with Eileen Davis at The Ohio State University with an emphasis in languages.
    - Ruth has taught voice since 1950.
    - Ruth is a member of the National Association of Teachers of Singing and has attended many of their seminars over the years.
    - Ruth also has experience in teaching voice to those who have damaged vocal cords.
    - Ruth also studied at the American Institute of Vocal Studies in Graz, Austria.
- Marise Petry
    - A lifelong singer and music lover. Marise began her musical studies at age of 5 with Beatrice Orr in Baltimore, Ohio. She often likes to say that she could read music before she could read words. Upon approaching the 7th grade, Mrs. Orr started training her formally in singing as well as continuing the piano.

- While attending Ohio University—Portsmouth Campus [now Shawnee State], she studied privately with Shirley Crothers.
- At the main campus of Ohio University in Athens, she studied with Diana Skentzos Alexander and Marjorie Stevenson, and earned her Bachelor of Music degree in Music Education with vocal emphasis and piano secondary. Upon graduation in 1975, she began teaching voice and piano as an independent teacher.
- In the 1990's Marise developed chronic bronchitis and resulting asthma. Due to excessive coughing associated with the disease, she damaged her voice and that is what led her to Ruth Manahan for study.

Why we wrote this book

- This book came about in response to a feeling that music today, especially singing, is starting to lose its beauty in tone. Eleanor Steber once said that in the modern teaching of voice there is more emphasis on volume than beauty of tone. One should never produce a tone at a volume that goes past its beauty.
- Eleanor Steber's influence will be obvious to those of you who are familiar with her approach to singing. It is in honor of her and to perpetuate this bel canto school of singing that we dedicate our work here.
- If asked what it is that we are unraveling, we would respond that it is the William Whitney-Eleanor Steber method of beauty over volume.
- We believe that the "bel canto" method is being tossed aside in favor of loud singing with no beauty. "Bel Canto" school is from Italy
  - This Italian method is over the top and floating while other methods in contrast are more of a straight line approach from the throat.
  - In Bel Canto the tone comes out of the energy, not pushed with the energy.
- In the course of our teacher/student relationship, the two of us have come to discover a kindred spirit in each other. We have been able to banter back and forth ways to communicate the same ideas in

different ways and to examine and study our own and our students' voices. We realized that there were many misconceptions that have come about over the years in vocal teaching or at least phrases and words that may be construed in ways not intended. We wanted to put down in writing our thoughts, discoveries, concepts and philosophies in hopes that other teachers and students of voice may find something contained here to be of value to their own study.

Who and when lessons help

- We believe that anyone with the desire can learn the concepts of singing.
- If pitch matching is the problem, the teacher could try the following. Use a tape recorder so that the student may practice in between lessons. Remember that it may take several months before real improvement is realized:
  - EXERCISE: Have the student sing any note of his/her choice. Then teacher locates that note on the keyboard. Use that note as the starting point calling it "do"
  - THE EXERCISE EXTENDED: Move to the "sol–do" concept. Work on "sol–do" in keys near the original comfortable key. With children, try the minor 3rds as suggested by the Kodály method. Gradually introduce the other notes of the scale.

How the teacher and the student can use the materials

- We invite you to use this book and its accompanying materials in whatever way best helps you for where your or your students' voices are and what they need at this moment in time. That may require you to take chapters and lessons out of sequence.
- We also invite you to use whatever helps you. If a particular concept, exercise or experiment does not help with the desired improvement, then discard it and try another.
- We have also left space for the teacher to include his/her own thoughts, exercises etc. and for students to make notes of any further thought they or their teacher has while exploring the different lessons here contained.

Upon studying voice

- Keep an open mind. You must <u>want</u> to change your sound and be willing to try new approaches and to sound differently than you presently do.
- Concentrate on your voice as an instrument, not on you the person. Our voices are such a personal part of us, that we often take criticism as a personal affront. We must be willing to extrapolate the voice from the person. For instance, when using a mirror, focus on your mouth, lips and cheeks (what is referred to as the embouchure in instruments). Do not look at your own eyes, unless you are ready to be objective about yourself and the mannerisms you may have that can interfere with vocal production.
- Be willing to make funny sounds and faces and to experiment.
- The use of a taping device can be quite helpful in practice as well as analyzing the voice.
- Be aware of what you are doing physically and the sensations.

DISCLAIMER

Over our years of training and teaching, we have been to countless vocal workshops, read many books and magazine articles about singing and the voice, and talked to many other teachers and students of voice. We wish acknowledge everyone who has influenced our approach to the teaching of singing. If we have included any concept or exercise or method that others believe they have originated and we have not cited as the source, we apologize and invite you to contact us so that proper acknowledgement can be made and included in the updating of this book and the web site.

CHAPTER ONE

The Body

LESSON ONE

Posture

POSTURE: All correct singing begins with proper posture.

POSTURE AFFECTS BREATHING CAPABILITY: Posture can either tighten or relax the rib cage. Correct posture enables breath to be taken in without tension. Think of two rubber bands, one old and rigid and the other new and easily expanded. Elasticity of the muscles allows for a deeper breath and the air to flow in freely. Good posture allows the chest to be naturally and comfortably high not stretched and tight or causing curvature of the back too far backward or too far forward. It is not the "chest up and tummy in" military stance.

OTHER EFFECTS OF POSTURE: If incorrect, posture can throw the neck forward, which is like a "kink in a hose" and blocks the passageway for air to flow up and therefore free vibration is not allowed or enabled. Posture affects the distribution of body weight. Good posture gives an illusion of confidence—which may lead to confidence.

THE ALEXANDER TECHNIQUE: There are many books and teachers available on the Alexander Technique. We advocate their position on posture, and we are attempting a brief overview, not an in depth study in this book. The following are the points we want to offer in this book: When lengthening the body, imagine that it happens from the tailbone to the top vertebrae at the back of the neck. Pull the rib cage up "out of the pelvis." Gently lift the head from the intersection of a line between the ears and line starting between the eyes going directly back. Note that we are using the term "lengthening" and not "stretching". "Stretching" could indicate a certain amount of tension and lead to a misunderstanding of what is being asked.

MISCONCEPTION: Stand up straight, that is "Shoulders back, chest out, stomach in."
- This military style stance would cause too much tension and place the center of gravity too far back.

BACK and SHOULDERS: Be sure that the shoulders are not pulled back, nor is the back arching in a position that pulls the weight backward. Instead, readjust the posture allowing for back expansion when inhaling.

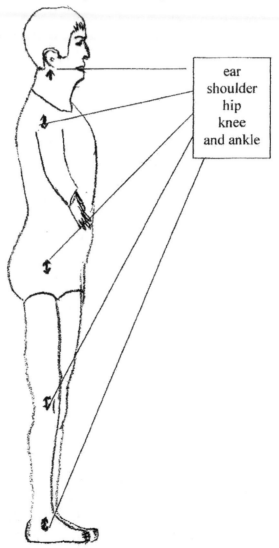

In proper posture, align the ear, shoulder hip, knee and ankle.

HEAD and NECK: Do not let the head jut forward, but draw head and neck straight back.

EXERCISE:
- With hands clasped behind the head, draw head back with hands remaining stationary creating some resistance. This will strengthen the neck muscles.

EXERCISE:
- Lower head forward and draw back with the neck. Hold the position for a count of "10". (Relax) Add a head turn to the left; hold for "10". (Relax) Then a head turn to the right, hold for "10". This exercise will help relax any tension in the neck.

EXERCISE:
- Clasp hands and place behind the head. Let the weight of your arms gently stretch the neck. This is another neck relaxation exercise.

FEET POSITION: Feet are positioned far enough apart so as not to feel off balance. One foot slightly advanced, and very slightly slanted outward. Position your weight forward over the arch of the foot. Caution, never lean back on your heels.

KNEES: Knees should not be "locked" stiffly into position, likewise not "over flexed." There is a feeling of "readiness to spring" in the knees, ready to move the body in any direction.

POSTURE CHECK ROUTINE

- Start at feet—be sure weight is distributed over the middle of the arches and just behind the balls of the feet.
- Soft, unlocked knees
- Tuck the pelvis under
- Lengthen from tailbone to base of the head.
- Align shoulders with hips
- Drawing the neck back, align ears with the shoulders; be sure that the chin is not jutted forward.

- Bend forward from hips, until there is a feeling of released tension in the chest with back in a position to expand when inhaling.
- Check weight distribution at feet again.

The teacher looks for . . .
- A gently lifted chest.
- An evenly positioned head, not leaning back on the neck and not bending forward and down, or chin tucked inward, or chin jutted forward.
- A straight-line look from head to toe. No bowed back or locked knees.
- The rib cage is lifted up, away from the waist, Not allowed to rest on the pelvis. The intercostal muscles must support the ribs up to keep them from sagging.

Additional Notes to teachers:
When you first observe a new student, be sure to analyze the posture. A skeleton model can help the student visualize proper body alignment.

PHYSICAL PROBLEMS THAT MIGHT AFFECT POSTURE

- One leg may be longer than the other. A chiropractor can diagnose and prescribe treatment.
- Observing a tightening in the neck and/or chest muscles can identify another problem. Student will feel a constriction of breath. Leaning forward from the hips just slightly enough to feel a relaxation in the chest, will release the tension and allow a better breath. Heels may need to be higher in order to better align the body. Try placing heels only on a raised surface, such as a book, and listen for any improved sound.

LESSON TWO

Posture And Tension Related To Posture

TENSION IN THE BODY: In order to sing with your full resonant voice, you must eliminate unwanted tensions in the body.

THE CHEST: The chest will be raised sufficiently if the lengthening of the spine is done correctly. We want a "comfortable lift". Lifting the chest should not cause the back to bow. There should be a feeling of broadening in the chest. This could also be described as "open chested."

TO RELIEVE CHEST TENSION

EXERCISE:
- Place hands on a stationary object (like a wall or piano) and lean into it. Then blow out on a "ssssss" intentionally tightening the chest (but not the throat). After exhaling all your air, relax and inhale (with an open throat.) The "S's" create a resistance as in an isometric exercise

EXERCISE:
- Inhale with a relaxed open throat; hold your breath as if you are still inhaling. Then slowly and gently blow out. Inhale again and sing the exercise or phrase you are working on.

EXERCISE:
- Lift the rib cage up, away from the waist. Do not allow it to rest on the pelvis. The intercostal muscles must support the ribs up to keep them from sagging.

THE ARMS: The arms, while relaxed, need to aid the chest in being expanded into the open chest position.

EXPERIMENT:
- For a moment stand hands cupped, palms up and one hand rested on the other. Hold elbows out and lift from the rib cage. Then, gently lower your hands to your side keeping what could be described as an "open chested" feeling.

THE SHOULDERS: There is a "T" position of shoulders and trunk of the body. Shoulders are relaxed and comfortably back.

EXPERIMENT:
- Try bending your arms at the elbows and then using your arms draw the shoulders back to align with the rest of your body Your arms and elbows will be parallel to the body, not drawn back beyond the body.. You will feel an opening up of the chest area. Drop the arms keeping the shoulders in the aligned position.

BODY WEIGHT DISTRIBUTION:
- Body weight is centered directly over the arch just behind the balls of the feet. This stance creates more stability than being farther forward on the foot. Notice that this is a different idea than the "traditional" stance of "on the balls of your feet." We observed this difference in consultation with a chiropractor and when we tried it, we found it to be more stabilizing and that it keeps our body in better alignment.
- For even weight distribution, avoid leaning back on the heels and think of a line going directly through the center of the body that divides into an inverted "Y" going on through the middle of the arches of the feet.

THE BACK: Back should be lifted up and expanding. Avoid drooping and pulling down of the trapezius muscles *[see the following diagram for their location.]* Be sure that the back is not bowed backward.

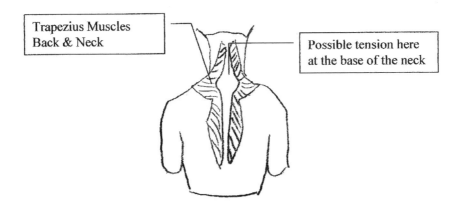

TIGHTNESS at the base of the neck. See the note in the above illustration.

Exercise:
- In Alexander—an exercise is to walk like a gorilla with head loose and arms swinging. Be sure to release the tension at the base of the skull so head is completely free.

LESSON THREE

Posture With Emphasis On Relaxation Of Muscles

POSTURE EXERCISES AND PHYSICAL WARM-UP ROUTINE: To encourage the muscles to relax, stretching is essential. Stretches are done slowly, gently and deliberately with smooth motion, not fast or jerking. The following exercises are good to do anytime, but especially before singing in the morning, or after a day of work or school.

CHOOSE FROM THE FOLLOWING BUT DO NOT DO THEM ALL AT ONE TIME, INSTEAD VARY YOUR ROUTINE.

FULL BODY STRETCHES

EXERCISE:
- Stretch up, arms up, reaching high.

EXERCISE:
- Bend over at waist and hips; relax and dangle. Again release the tension at the base of the skull.

EXERCISE:
- Cat Stretch. In bent over position, bow the back and stretch like a cat. Then gently "roll" the body back up, thinking vertebrae, by vertebrae.

EXERCISE:
- Shoulder Rolls and Shrugs
    Both forward/backward
    Right forward/backward

Left forward/backward
Shrug shoulders slowly up then down

EXERCISE:
- Lateral stretch
    Face forward and lightly anchor one hand to a stationary object, like a pole or a doorway, at shoulder level.
    Gradually turn your body around to face as forward as you can without causing pain. Hold.
    Return to starting position and repeat with other hand and turning in the opposite direction..

HEAD AND NECK STRETCHES

EXERCISE:
- Head turning
    Head center
    Turn and look over right shoulder. Hold.
    Back to center
    Turn and look over left shoulder. Hold.

EXERCISE:
- Neck relaxation and extension
    With hands clasped and palms to back of head, gently bow head down using the weight of your arms to extend the stretch.

EXERCISE:
- To relieve tension at the back of the neck, bottom of the head, lean over, stretch like a cat. When you arch your back, lower your head in full relaxation. Let the weight of your head gently elongate your neck.

EXERCISE:
- Isometric neck and head exercise

    o With right hand, press your head on the right side and counter with pressure from your head and neck.
    o With left hand, press you head on the left side and counter with pressure from your head and neck.

SIDE STRETCHES

EXERCISE:
- Basic side stretch
    Place left arm over your head, grab your left wrist with your right hand
    Bend to the right side
    Place right arm over your head, grab your right wrist with your left hand
    Bend to the left side
- Add a twist
    Same as above, but twist the trunk of the body about a quarter turn.

FACE

Toning and relaxing face muscles helps to prepare for vowel formation. Facial exercises give overall tone to facial muscles and allows for relaxation, getting rid of tension.

EXERCISE:
- Massage the jaw line from tip of ears to center of the chin using fingertips tracing small circles.

EXERCISE:
- "Bunny rabbit" style nose wrinkle; move nose up and down to strengthen the muscle of the cheek and nose area. These muscles are used in a lifted manner that will put the sound forward and up into resonators and will help high notes. It helps to avoid a "drooping" look to the face.

EXERCISE:
- Move eyebrows up and down. This will give one an "alive, euphoric" feeling.

EXERCISE:
- Chew like a cow on its cud. Over emphasize the movements. This relaxes the jaw.

Exercise:
- Open your mouth as wide as you can and then follow by scrunching up your face. This exercise help to give face a full range of motion easily.

Exercise:
- Roll eyeballs around in a circle.

Exercise:
- Make a grin like the "Cheshire cat", showing teeth; tighten jaw and neck muscles, then let go of the tension and relax.

Exercise:
- Suck in the cheeks, all the way back to the back teeth. Strengthening the cheek muscles contributes to the formation of a very focused and pure "OH".

Exercise:
- Stick tongue out as far as possible to one side and turn head only as far as possible to that same side. Then repeat on the other side.

LESSON FOUR

Posture Of The Voice

THE LARYNX: The larynx should always be in a low position. Proper low position of the larynx will result in more space in the back of the mouth and throat, allowing the tongue to relax in a forward, not swallowed position.

EXPERIMENT: Locating proper position of the larynx:
- Place hand gently on Adam's apple and yawn. You will feel the larynx go to the proper position.
- Another way to locate proper position: Gently drop your head back, open your mouth, move your tongue forward and breathe in and out and yawn.

CONCEPT
THE CRANIAL LIFT

We developed this concept while trying to find a way to avoid the dropped jaw look that gives a downward feel to the skull. In order to position the vocal mechanism properly and to create an open space for the purpose of voice to resonate we advocate approaching this opening of space using a "cranial lift." Our concept of "cranial lift" involves a lifting of the cranium especially from the middle of the head to the back.

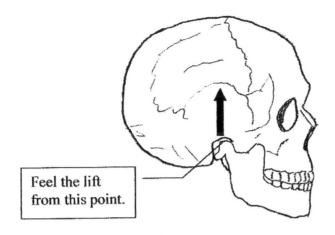

Illustration of the Craniel Lift

EXPERIMENT:
- Move your jaw side to side and feel with your fingers the place where the jaw connects to the skull. If you lower your jaw, you will feel a sort of "hole".
- Now from that position, lift the cranium, as happens when you yawn, (see the arrow in illustration above) separating it from the jaw at the ears and feeling the lifted feeling on toward the back of the head. The previous "hole" will now be experienced as flattened.
- Note that if you are raising your eyebrows, you are too far forward in your lift. You will feel the lift at the center and back of the head. It will give a lengthening effect of the back of the neck.
- It is a beginning of a yawn, but not in the center back of the mouth. Instead, it is at the sides of upper head (or cranium).
- Be sure the upper lip is not drawing down covering the top front teeth, yet avoid a very tense lifted upper lip.

THE ADVANTAGE TO USING A CRANIAL LIFT

- This "cranial lift" shows an alertness and vitality without <u>raising the eyebrows</u>.
- The end result is a relaxed jaw, space in mouth and throat, and the relaxed positioning of the tongue. With this position, one can sing the full range of the voice without changes in the tone quality. It

also keeps the voice from dropping too low, preventing the return to high notes.

EXPERIMENT:
- Combine the cranial lift with a narrowing of the cheeks as in saying an exaggerated (British accent) "OH" bringing the lips slightly forward. The sound can be described as open and uninhibited as well as focused or narrowed.

MISCONCEPTION: "Drop the jaw."

DEFINITION: Dropped jaw is opening the mouth by the lowering of the jawbone.
- If one merely "drops the jaw" you will indeed open your mouth, but there is a downward perception associated with this phrase. When one thinks in a downward direction, the tone has a tendency to drop too low and is prevented from attaining the ability to go from the very lowest notes to the highest notes in the range.
- Only thinking of dropping the jaw makes the face appear dull and frowning. It may also result in a "spread" and "thin" sound; in other words with too much space side to side and not enough up and down.
- The term "Open your mouth" also does not get at the basic lift and openness that is desired for optimum sound. Instead, it closes the throat.
- Notice particularly when changing from any vowel to "oh, ah or aw" one tends to drop the jaw. This will "drop" the tone and tighten the tongue, closing off the back of the throat. Notice also the change in the jaw at the ear as described in the explanation of the cranial lift above.

EXERCISE: [USE "OH-AY"]

Refer to the vocal exercise # 1 in Appendix of this book.

CHAPTER TWO

Breathing

LESSON ONE
Locate The Breath

MISCONCEPTION: "Deep Breath"

- Too often the term "deep breath" implies raising the shoulders, thrusting out the chest and bowing the back.
- A deep breath refers to a full breath, using the abdominal muscles.

ABDOMINAL BREATHING

- Proper breathing for singing and breath control involves the expansion of the rib cage all around the body.
- As the lungs expand, there will also be an expansion of the rib cage front to back, side to side.

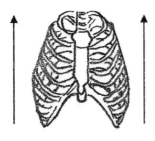 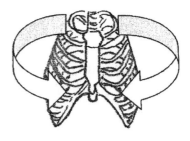

WRONG CORRECT

Do not raise up the body when inhaling Expand all around the body when inhaling

THE DIAPHRAGM

- The term "diaphragm" in anatomy refers to a muscular membranous partition separating the abdominal and thoracic cavities and functioning in respiration.
- The diaphragm is the muscle used to draw in air, that is, to inhale. The diaphragm gives the lungs room to expand and when the lungs expand, the contents of the abdomen below the diaphragm will move down and forward The physical proof of this is the expansion of the abdominal area. (Easy, non-technical way to explain is that when you inhale your "stomach" goes out.) The model below is often used in science classes to illustrate the action of the diaphragm.

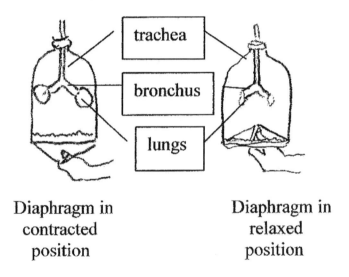

Diaphragm in contracted position

Diaphragm in relaxed position

- Again, as the lungs expand, there will also be an expansion of the rib cage front to back and side to side.
- In the end, breath is felt all around the trunk, from the back, under the arms and all the way down to the pelvic region.

DEFINITION: To breathe refers to inhaling.

MISCONCEPTION "Diaphragmatic breathing"

- The diaphragm is not <u>where</u> we breathe <u>from</u>, but <u>the muscle</u> that enables inhalation to occur.
- It is an involuntary muscle, meaning that it works automatically. That is, we do not have to think to breathe.

EXPERIMENT:
- Lay down on your back. 1) Place a book just above the waist; breathe in with a relaxed breath. The book will move up upon inhalation and down upon exhalation. The shoulders and chest remain relatively still. 2) Now, using pursed lips draw in the air slowly as if sipping from a straw (raising the book). Then blow the air out slowly (lowering the book). 3) Return to a standing position and now without the book, try to repeat the same breathing technique. Shoulders and chest remain still.

EXERCISE:
- Blow through pursed lips, as if blowing out a candle. Blow in groups of two. Be aware of the abdominal muscle action. Blow upward as opposed to blowing bearing downward and collapsing the body.

EXERCISE [NOT SUNG]:
- Using an exaggerated whisper, say the word "Hook", elongating the "h" a little, and saying: "Hook, hook, hook, *(rest)* . . . Hook, hook, hook *(rest)* . . . Hook, hook, hook *(rest)*. [Note to the teacher: in a few people the "k" will cause tightness in the throat. In that case, try "hoo hoo hoo hoo . . ." It may be the tongue is drawing back]

EXERCISE:
- Refer to the vocal exercise # 6 in Appendix of this book. Use "Hoh" or "Hook"

EXERCISE [NOT SUNG]:
- Pant like a dog. Start slowly and deliberately. Then increase the speed until it is repeated evenly and easy to continue. Lie down if this is difficult when standing.

LESSON TWO-A

Inhale

In proper inhalation, one expands the thorax (chest and upper abdominal muscles, ribs up to under the arms and the back) and air rushes in to fill the vacuum. It is incorrect to "suck in" the air as if using a straw to make that expansion happen.

MISCONCEPTION:
Actually, "breathe" means to *pull* air in. Actually, "breathe" or "take a breath" means to inhale. Use the following tips:

- <u>Let the breath in</u>, don't pull it in. Inhaling should not require a great effort.
- Avoid having the tongue drop down into the back of the throat which will take up space and close up the breathing passage.
- Allow the throat to open (as opposed to <u>making</u> it open).

RELAX

- Let the breath in through the mouth; do not pull in the breath.
- "Release" thinking, "let go". The body lets go, but there is a measure of readiness. Be careful not to drop the lower abdomen or shoulders. The chest remains up through the whole process of inhaling and singing. Note that this drop of the abdomen could be caused by a lack of muscle tone. In this latter case, imagine lengthening the body from within while taking a breath avoiding a jerking drop of the lower abdomen.
- Release under the arms and chest. Sometimes this is hampered by a fear of coughing (especially in the case of asthmatics or those recovering from a respiratory infection.)

- Check to be sure that the back muscles are not pulling down [you may wish to refer back to Chapter 1: Lesson 2 concerning THE BACK]. Lean a little forward from the waist until you can feel expansion in your upper back as you inhale. If your body is "swayed back", the back muscles especially the trapezoids, will pull down on inhalation and there is little back expansion.
- Be sure to have an open throat. Think an "OH" shape going all the way from top to bottom of the windpipe. The breath will be a quiet one.

EXPERIMENT:
- Position arms outstretched directly in front of the body. With mouth open and throat in a relaxed yawning position quickly bring arms out to the side in a horizontal position when doing this expand the full circumference of the body. Do not pull in breath. On expansion the lungs will fill. Exhale and bring arms back to original position. Exhale <u>slowly</u> to a hissing sound coordinating with the arms returning slowly to the front. This will train muscles to control the slow exhale needed for singing and singing long phrases on one breath easily.

CONCEPT: "Open the Throat"

This phrase refers to the feeling of space as one breathes and/or sings. It involves both the relaxation of the tongue, the lowering of the larynx, and the lifting of the soft palate.

EXPERIMENT:
- Drop your head back gently looking at the ceiling. Open your mouth and relax your tongue in a forward position. Feel the open throat and the breathing sensation of air moving in and out in a normal breathing pattern. The beginning of a yawn is the moment when you are relaxing and lowing the larynx. The open throat will help the air to come in naturally, not forced. The lowering of the larynx and the relaxed open throat will also prepare your voice to begin singing. Be cautious that the back of the neck is not too tight.

EXPERIMENT:
- Another method of opening up the throat is to breathe in thinking the air going "up" before going down, much like smelling your favorite smell (a rose, apple pie, etc)

EXERCISE:
- Blow out your air until there is none left, then allow your body to "let go and relax" and allow lungs to fill up with air naturally. Be careful to maintain a certain amount of energy and do not allow the lower abdominal muscles drop.
- You may want to practice by stopping between phrases in a song to completely blow out all your breath and then follow with the feeling of a relaxed and "full body" breath. This will allow your body to get used to the idea of releasing any tension and then inhaling naturally.

EXPERIMENT:
- This experiment will help the student differentiate a relaxed, open throat, from any tension in the air passage. Instruction: "Hold your breath." In the way one normally does, there is a gripping feeling in the throat. "Now, hold your breath by keeping your abdominal muscles in the position they are at the end of inhalation and relaxing your throat." This will call to the student's attention the muscles that are engaged in the breathing and breath support system.

EXERCISE
- With both hands straight out, push against the teacher's hands, or a wall or a stationary object. Notice the abdominal firming. The throat and neck muscles should remain relaxed.

LESSON TWO-B

Inhale (continued)

MISCONCEPTION

Grab the breath, or suck in the breath and then hold it until you're ready to sing.

- One does <u>not</u> need to take, grab or gasp for breath, but instead breathe in naturally, letting the air fill the vacuum in the lungs.
- One does <u>not</u> need to hold the breath even momentarily before beginning the tone or phrase. If you do stop, there is a tightening that happens and often causes the larynx to go to a higher position.

GIVE YOURSELF TIME TO INHALE

- It is important to take your time to inhale; in fact, you usually have more time than you think you do. If you do not think you have time, you may be holding on the last note of the previous phrase too long. You must <u>give</u> yourself time.
- You are allowed to take a little time value off the note or rest preceding a breath so as to have time to breathe, especially for up-coming long phrases.
- <u>Do</u> be sure to end the phrase lightly so as not to accent the note before the breath, unless the composer wants that note accented.
- Taking time is also a part of letting go.
- Gasping for air and then holding it in before beginning the tone will cause a gripping feeling in the throat and the tongue to draw backwards. [More on the tongue later. See Chapter 3]

Experiment:
- Think of inhaling and exhaling as a continuous circle. Using one arm and hand, scribe a circle a) going from front beginning at chest height and circling downward the toward the back heading upward b) over the top, and then c) back to front heading downward. As your hand draws down to the bottom of the circle, exhale. As your hand slowly continues the circle upward from the back, inhale slowly using the "letting go" and "open throat" concepts as above, until your hand reaches the top of the circle. Then, without stopping to hold your breath think of it as "turning around" and going right into the exhale. Exhale as your hand comes back to the front and reaches the bottom of the circle. Then you may pause and repeat. You might refer to this as a circular breathing technique.
- Variation: If you wish, you may do the same experiment as above, this time exhale much slower than you inhaled; you may choose to use a lightly aspirated "ssss" sound. At the same time, be sure you are slowing down the descent of your hand.

The teacher looks and listens for . . .
- The "noisy" breath. The throat is not open in this case or the tongue is cutting off the air passage or perhaps time has not been taken to inhale.
- Inability to have enough breath to finish a phrase.
  - It could be that the student did not take time to breathe, or to "let go"
  - It could be that the student's lips and mouth lose focus or roundness and when that happens, breath is lost.
  - A third problem could be using too much air somewhere in the phrase; perhaps too much air used on initiating the phrase or consonant, or too heavy on a tone
  - Slow articulation of the initial consonant or a lateness of the vowel can cause a loss of breath as well as giving the impression that the note is late. This may be just an instant too long, but long enough to use too much breath.
  - Lost control of the breath. See the Chapter 2 Lesson 4 on breath control
  - Singer may have taken too much air for the previous phrase and therefore did not have enough lung space for the fresh breath.

- Listen for the sound of the epiglottis beginning the first tone, especially if it begins on a vowel sound. This sound is like the beginning of a cough. This is called a "glottal attack". The student may be holding their breath after inhaling.
- Check for an arched back or leaning backward posture. It is difficult to get a full breath if the posture of the back and/or trunk of the body is wrong. See Chapter 1, Lesson 1

LESSON THREE

Exhale and Sing

BEGINNING THE FIRST TONE OF THE PHRASE [the Attack]

- If one has inhaled in the "mold of the vowel", then one should produce the tone from a gently rounded lip position.
- What does to find the "mold of the vowel mean? The lips are a bit forward and rounded with the placement of the tone focuses on the hard palate (or roof of the mouth). Use a vocal exercise on the vowels "ee-oh" rapidly repeating the alternate vowels on a single pitch similar to Exercise # 2 in Appendix. This will develop a feel for the vowel mold. which is the formation of lips and cheeks that allows for the least amount of movement and change in tone between two vowels.
- The tone begins on the breath; with an open throat, tongue forward.
- Referring back to the idea of 'circular' breathing . . . (see Chapter 2, Lesson 2-B experiment) breathe in (in the mold of the vowel) then 'turn the breath around' and begin the note, exhaling slowly and controlled. The larynx should be in a low position, but not pushed down.
- Always keep the breath 'active'. <u>Keep blowing</u> while you sing. And keep the breathing muscles involved in the singing.
- If it feels like you've "locked" your chest upon inhalation before beginning the tone, try releasing a little bit of air, then sing . . . This could be thought of as being like a silent "h".

EXPERIMENT:
- Lean head back, open your mouth and sticking your tongue out, slowly breathe in and out and feel the back of the throat "drop". That is also the feeling of the larynx dropping gently and slowly. Then sing 5 notes in a descending scale [sol, fa, mi, re, do] on "Oh" or "Aw" as in Exercise #5 in Appendix.

EXERCISE:
- The following exercise will help in the avoidance of the glottal attack (mentioned in Chapter 2 Lesson 2-B). Begin with an "h" sound and then again with "h" being silent. Begin the attack on "oh" with the same feeling of open throat, beginning the tone on the breath. Use repeated tones in a comfortable range using the pattern: ‖:quarter-note, quarter-rest, quarter-note, quarter-rest:‖ whole-note. See Exercise #6 in Appendix.

EXERCISE:
- "The 3 sip exercise"
  The purpose of this exercise is: To get the breathing muscles to expand and be more flexible; you will then get more air using the back and side muscles; and the bone structure gets used to accommodating this expansion.

    1) Sip in a little air. Stop and hold.
    2) Sip in a 2nd time. Stop and hold.
    3) Sip in a 3rd time. Stop and hold.
    4) Then, blow out all the air rapidly, with lips pursed. Do not collapse the body particularly do not let the rib cage collapse inward.
    5) Then relax and let the air come in naturally. Do not collapse the rib cage, but let it remain high so that the air can come in freely without having to work harder to expand the rib cage.

  Sing the "Oh-Ay" Exercise #1 in Appendix.

CONCEPT:

The chest should remain lifted during the singing process of inhale, sing, let go, inhale. A dropped chest will decrease the space in the chest cavity and cause extra work to move it on inhalation.

PROBLEM—NOT ENOUGH AIR:

- Check for consonants that have taken too long. Consonants should not be held on to, but quickly articulated. The exception is when consonants are used for "effect" as in a choir performance.
- Was too much air taken in the previous phrase that is not used? Air needs to be used before a good breath can be taken to replace it.
- With practice it will become automatic to get the correct amount of breath.

THREE STEPS IN TEACHING BREATHING:

These steps indicate an order of steps in which to develop full breathing.

>Step one: Find the breath with the abdomen extending on inhale and contracting on exhale.
>Step two: Releasing but not dropping, the lower abdominal muscles to allow for a fuller breath.
>Step three: Use the back and underarm expansion.

LESSON FOUR
Breath Control And Support

MISCONCEPTION

"Sing from the Diaphragm"

- This term should NOT refer to the diaphragm as a muscle, but more often is used to indicate a general area of the body, namely the abdominal region.

WHAT IS BREATH CONTROL/SUPPORT?

DEFINITION:
- When we use the terms breath control or breath support in this book, we are referring to the use of the breathing muscles (abdominal, side, back) as one sings, keeping the tone vibrant and alive. It gives it an impression that the notes are moving forward. Forward motion describes an energy that keeps the tone from sounding stagnant.
- Think 3 tiers of support. 1) The very low below-the-belly-button area 2) Waist area 3) Ribs including the intercostal muscles [those muscles between the ribs] which help to keep the ribs expanded. Within the rib area are other controlling muscles—the side abdominal muscles and the "energy" button [See Chapter 2, Lesson 5].
- Imagine an inflated balloon. As air is <u>slowly</u> released, the balloon does not suddenly collapse, but the walls of the balloon gradually retreat.

THINGS TO REMEMBER:

- Support the breath by gradually and gently pulling the abdomen <u>in</u>, <u>not up</u>. Pulling the abdomen up will tighten the chest.

- Try to "activate" and then "reactivate" the muscles. The idea is to get in contact with those muscles and know how to use them.
- Make the breath work for you. If the breath is standing still, you're losing air, not conserving it. Keep blowing through the phrase. Use a certain amount of resistance in the trunk of the body . . . not the tongue.
- Think of your breath-flow like a water fountain. Don't let the water "dribble" out, but let it continue as a steady breath pressure to support the tone.
- The tone floats on the breath as if it were a light ball above a tube of flowing air
- Pull in at the belly button.

EXERCISE:
- Blow against your fist. The exhaling force or resistance will be with the abdominal muscles. Be sure to relax your throat and tongue, keeping the airway open.

EXERCISE:
- With abdominal muscles, pull in, pull up, and relax. This will help tone the lower abdominal muscles—good for anyone who lacks muscle tone in the abdomen.

EXPERIMENT:
- Place your thumbs in your side, under the rib cage. When abdominal muscles are not engaged, you can push your thumbs in easily. When abdominal muscles ARE engaged, you can feel the firming of the abdominal muscles, which will resist the thumbs' attempt to press inward.

EXPERIMENT:
- Imagine that your legs are "rooted" into the floor, in much the same way as a tree is rooted into the ground. In this way, your leg muscles contribute to the support of the tone. One foot should be slightly forward of the other.

NOTE: Once muscles are strong and toned, then you don't have to think support all the time, but think energy. One can over tighten the muscles causing tension, which is also undesirable and affects the tone in other ways.

Exercise:
- The "ee-oh-no" Exercise #7 in Appendix.
  Re-support or energize each "EE" [after the first one] and release on "no".

Over time this exercise will help you hold the sound "up" and keep from going under pitch. It will help keep the same energy level throughout a long note.

Experiment:
- When going higher in pitch, people tend to pull the support up. To correct this, put your arms straight out in front of you and when you start to sing higher notes, bring your arms downward. A slightly different approach would be to press down on a tabletop while singing, which will help you avoid stretching for the high pitch.

EXTENDING THE BREATH:

- No whooshing of air, sighing or breathiness
- Sing softly, but keep the intensity
- Keep ribs expanded as you sing. Then when you need to take a breath, the ribs are already extended outward and only the air needs to rush in as you relax the breathing muscles.

Exercise:
- Refer to exercise #4 in the Appendix keeping in mind the following: re-support and lighten on the "Oh". Repeat where marked with the goal being 15 times the pattern before the descending scale. This repeated area is always light and high in the head. It is very important to keep the "OH" up and light; do not let it drop or become heavy. Also, do not change markedly between "ee" and "Oh". In other words, wrap the OH around the EE.
- The use of a rubber exercise band can help firm abs and breathing muscles.

Exercise:
- An isometric exercise like the following will also help develop support. Press palm-to-palm, student to teacher, and feel the abdominal muscles contract in support.

LESSON FIVE

Breath Control And Energy

CONCEPT:
THE ENERGY BUTTON

- We refer to the muscles just below the breastbone as the "energy button." It is here that the vibrancy of the tone is produced. You may have heard the expression "sing from your gut" as a way to get at this energy.
- When using the energy button, let go mentally and let it do its work.
- Use the side abdominal muscles as well as low abdominal muscles and the energy button.
- The energy button connects with the phonation. It needs to be locked in from the beginning to the end. The tone floats on the energy of the breath.

OTHER THINGS THAT AFFECT ENERGY

- If you hold your eyebrows up, you lose energy.
- Legs help support the tone. Imagine your legs rooted into the floor (like tree roots) and with a readiness to spring into action. This readiness exudes energy upward to the trunk of the body.
- Feel energy of the mind and the body.
- Sing <u>from</u> the energy. Using energy prevents a pushed volume and prepares the mind to be excited and ready. Think of "skipping" versus "jumping" a rope; or "play" versus "work".
- Some other visualizations might include: a clock spring, or wind up toy which when wound stores energy. You need to "wind up" your mind and feel the energy in your body.

EXPERIMENT:
- Pick up a chair and sing. This will help connect the breathing muscles.

EXPERIMENT:
- Imagine a tire with an inner tube. The inner tube being the deep muscles those behind the rib cage as well as those just below the breastbone. The tire is the abdominal muscles. The inner tube is pliable while the tire is less flexible. Pull in at the energy button as you as you sing Exercise #6 in Appendix.

OTHER THOUGHTS ON ENERGY:

- Boiling water—from the heated water comes the bubbles (a.k.a. energy)
- Sound is propelled, not forced. Like a canon ball, or an arrow. The energy comes from the source—canon, bow.
- A ski jumper builds energy going downhill, but while in the air he is only floating out of the energy. Likewise, energy is the breath support and the tone floats on top of the energy. The sound is effortless, yet vibrant.
- Imagine a parachute, the air supports it. A parachute has no energy of its own. It is a floppy piece of cloth, but in receiving the air that supports it, it is given fullness, body and shape.
- When we're focused only on our abs for support, we often lose sight of whole body energy and the energy that exudes outward from within. The abdominal muscles work out of the energy; they do not make the energy.
- There's a certain amount of confidence that goes into energy . . . confidence, singing with feeling, being animated.
- *Add your own . . .*

PROPER BREATH SUPPORT WILL HELP PROJECT THE SOUND.

DEFINITION:
The word "project" refers to a sort of "megaphone" effect that resonates. It may be described as sending the sound "Out" instead of holding the sound "In" or singing to oneself. To project will make the sound louder,

but will not use a tight throat to make it loud. It is also called facemask resonance.

EXERCISE:
- This is a Face Mask Resonance Exercise from The Ohio State University Otolaryngology Department.
  - *Um-Hum* . . .
  - *Um-Hum ONE* . . . *Um-Hum TWO [continue up to ten]*

CONCEPT:

Now, combine facemask resonance with openness in the back, soft palate up, tongue forward. The sound cannot just stop at the facemask. One can focus too hard and loud in the mask and therefore it gives a pushing and too nasal a sound. The soft palate must be raised for the floating tone to happen.

CHAPTER THREE

The Tongue

LESSON ONE

"Taming The Shrewish Tongue" The Tongue As A Hinderance To Vocal Production

- The tongue is a larger muscle than most people think it is. See illustration below.
- An uncontrollable tongue will cause vocal problems
- When training a voice that has sung in the low register nearly exclusively, as the teacher tries to help extend the range upward there may be a large tongue problem, in that the tongue is pulled way back. The voice has not experienced the head voice tones.
- Do not confuse pulling back the tongue for or with lowering the larynx.

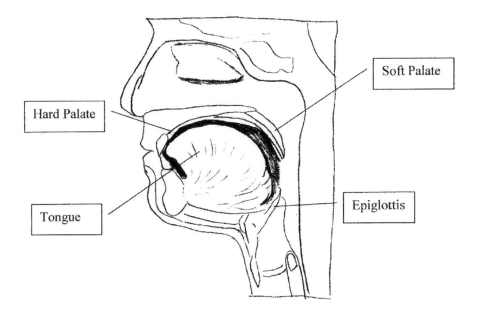

Notice the size and shape of the tongue in this illustration.

MISCONCEPTION

- To "open the throat" doesn't mean pull the tongue back and down in a full yawn or swallowing position.

PROPER POSITIONING OF THE TONGUE

- The proper tongue position will contribute to good vocal production.
- Keep the tongue in the forward position that it is in when saying the "a" as in "cat".
- The tongue arches at the molars and lies relaxed touching the inside surfaces of the teeth.
- The tongue should be forward from the back; but couple that with the support from the belly button area and the intercostals muscles (ribs in your sides and under the rib cage).

EXPERIMENT:
- Using a craft stick (or tongue depressor), gently lay the stick on the front half of the tongue. Then gently pull the stick forward bringing with it the tongue. Feel the effect of the forward tongue and how it opens the back of the throat. It may seem that the tongue is taking up more space in the mouth, in reality it opens up space in the back of the mouth. Try saying the long vowel sounds: "ay, ee, i, oh, u". If your tongue is fighting you and wants to pull on the craft stick, then your tongue is not relaxed. Keep working on this until the tongue remains relaxed and still.

EXERCISE:
- HuNG on a <u>single pitch</u>; then on <u>do, re, mi, re, do</u>; and on <u>do, re, mi, fa, sol, fa, mi, re, do</u>. See Exercise #49, #10 and #11, substituting "huNG" for "oo" in Appendix. "HuNG" is meant to indicate the "NG" sound as in the word "Hung" It helps to enunciate the "hu" and then go quickly to the "NG" as the main sound for the exercise.

EXERCISE:
- Over emphasize the "Bl" sticking your tongue out as you say: ||: **"Bla, Bla, Bla, Bla, Bla"** :|| (a as in cat). The exercise also loosens the lips.

EXERCISE:
- Saying "AW-YAW" repeatedly, on one pitch. There should be no jaw movement, only the tongue moves on the "y". See Exercise #50 in Appendix.

EXERCISE:
- On a single pitch, keep jaw still and sing very slowly and connected the syllables "Doh loh noh loh doh" emphasizing the tongue motion only, no jaw movement.

TONGUE TENSION

Many of the problems with the tongue are caused by tension. Try the following experiments to relieve tongue tension.

EXPERIMENT:
- The tongue should feel heavy of its own weight, not from a tension of trying to pull or push it down. Try a "dumb" face (Duh). Touch the back of the front teeth and touch the back of all the lower teeth. The tongue should lie in your mouth "like a piece of raw liver." Or, imagine a partially filled water balloon lying on your hand and the way it conforms to the shape of your palm and lies heavy and relaxed.

EXPERIMENT:
- Place the back of your hand lightly under the chin to check for tension. Swallow. Feel the tongue press down on your hand. Then, notice if the tongue does the same pressing down when you sing a single note with "ay, ee, ah, oh, oo". If it does, you are experiencing tongue tension.

On an "OH" the tongue needs to relax all the way to its base.

EXERCISE:
- Stick your tongue out, just saying the vowels "ay, ee, ah, oh, oo." Notice what happens at the base of the tongue and the muscles surrounding it. Hopefully when done successfully with very little tension, it will feel as if the throat has a big gaping hole in it. Now

sing a 5-five scale using "OH". After this exercise, a residual feeling of relaxation should be noticed.
- With sides of the tongue held gently in place by the back teeth say: "Kee, Kay, Kaw, Koh, Koo" Then release the tongue and repeat in the same manner. This exercise helps to produce a smoother vowel transition.

EXERCISE:
- Look in a mirror. Let your tongue relax and mold to the bottom of your mouth, looking spread out and relatively flat. Now work slowly speaking the vowels "OH" to "OO" keeping the tongue relatively still.

EXERCISE:
Using the following exercise regularly should strengthen the back of the tongue.
- Again looking in a mirror say the following, keeping the tongue in the "a" as in "cat" position:

First set:
  "Cat" *(repeat 3 times)*
  "Kate" *(repeat 3 times)*
  "Kee" *(repeat 3 times)*

Second set:
  "Cat-Koh" *(repeat 3 times)* Try to use the lips only and very little tongue changing. Also try to keep the tongue in contact with the upper back teeth, making you more aware of any tongue movement.

  "Kee-Koo" *(repeat 3 times)*

Third set:
  "Kitty, Kitty, Cat" *(repeat 3 times)*

LESSON TWO

"The Martyr Tongue"

BREATH SUPPORT & THE TONGUE

- Imagine the tongue saying: "If you're not going to support your breath properly, I'll just have to do it *sigh*"
- Support and phonation must co-ordinate or tongue will be forced to do something "bad"—probably a glottal attack and cutting off the throat.
- Remember that the tongue "acts up" whenever something else goes wrong.

THE TONGUE PLACEMENT AFFECTS INHALING

- If the tongue is pulled back and not in the "a" as in "cat" position, inhaling will be noisy and tense.
- When the tongue is in the wrong position upon intake of breath, then it will probably not be in the correct position to begin singing.
- [The following idea comes from student Laurie Steele] Making the tongue adjustment during breathing and before singing can be compared to a batter in baseball; the batter is prepared to swing by having the bat drawn back and ready; it does not make sense to prepare the swing with the bat in the position that is partially forward, then swinging after the pitch has been thrown as if to push the ball, not hit it. Likewise it does not make sense to adjust the tongue at the point where vocalization starts.

EXPERIMENT: Pant, breathe, sing any phrase. Repeat several times. This can result in a relaxed tongue, space in the back of your throat, a lifted soft palate and relaxation down through the body. This can help with openness and freedom of tone. NOTE: We have been amazed by the overall freedom and relaxation that we've felt when using this panting experiment.

MISCONCEPTION:

From the traditional chart of vowels on the tongue, one can infer that the tongue moves a lot on vowel changes. Too often one makes too much of a change when singing vowels.

EXPERIMENT: Again, try sticking your tongue out and say all the vowels without the tongue wiggling in and out. [eh, ee, ah, oh, oo]

THE TONGUE AND CONSONANTS

The tongue will move on the following consonants: d, g, j, k, l, n, q, s, t, x, z as well as gr, kl, pr, st, th. Try the tongue twister "Tip of the tongue to the top of the teeth" as a reminder of using the tongue on percussive consonants.

MISCONCEPTION:

Two misconceptions of how the tongue lays in the mouth are that the tongue is 1) in a "U" shape or 2) that it is pulled down, exposing the back of the throat.

- When looking for tongue problems look for the following: tongue is too narrow or flat or it's in a "U" shape or it is pulling back.
- The correct placement of the tongue is in the "a" position (as in cat). It is forward in the mouth and relaxed. It is relaxed and touching the inside of the teeth, even the teeth in the back.

TENSION AND THE TONGUE

- Tension tends to go to the tongue. Good breath support is one cure for tongue tension.
- Check shoulder and arm tension, which can also cause tongue tension.
- A tense tongue can contribute to a "dropped" sound; that is, too heavy and bearing down on the vocal folds.

CHAPTER FOUR

Tone Quality

LESSON ONE-A

Vocal Placement—The Floating Tone

WHAT IS "VOCAL PLACEMENT" AND WHY DO WE USE THE TERM IN THIS BOOK?

There is some controversy about the use of the term "vocal placement". You cannot take the voice and place it somewhere else, but in the context of visualization and feeling vibrations in different places the term is one way to describe those feelings.

WHAT ARE SOME OF THE VISUALIZATIONS WE USE TO DESCRIBE VOCAL PLACEMENT:

- Think of the space as high in the head, not low in the throat.
- The sound mushrooms up into the sinuses.
- Imitate a whiney tone of a little girl saying, "I don't want to do that!" This will help find a high placement in the mask of the face.

EXPERIMENT:
- Imagine putting a pencil across mouth and then sing "above" the pencil line.

EXPERIMENT:
- Do a soft, light snore. Feel the placement of the sound.

EXERCISE:
- Do a high, exhilarating sound of "Whoopee!"

EXERCISE: Start on a high note of your choice. Then glissando to a note an octave below by singing "Whooooo"

EXERCISE: Start on a note of your choice in the middle to lower range of your voice. Then imitate the sound of a siren sliding up and down in pitches.

DEFINITION OF FALSE VOCAL CORD IS FROM MEDICINENET.COM

False vocal cord: A fold of mucous membrane covering muscle in the larynx. The false vocal cord separates the ventricle of the larynx from the vestibule [entrance] of the larynx. Also called the false vocal fold. The purpose of the false vocal chords is to lubricate the true vocal cords.

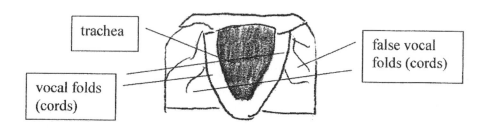

The false vocal cords can press against the true vocal cords and cause a tone that does not conform to the concept of a free tone. See the picture above for what and where the false vocal cords are located and then practice the exercise that follows to release the tension of the false vocal cords.

EXERCISE: THIS EXERCISE COMES FROM THE OTOLARGARLOGY & VOCAL THERAPY DEPARTMENT OF THE OHIO STATE UNIVERSITY

- Release the False Vocal Cords

    1. Arms down and bent at the elbow. Thumbs up and grunt hard.
    2. Hands go up and open, while you take in a quiet breath.
    3. Then in a "little girl's voice" say "Hee-hee-hee-hee-hee . . ." bringing the hands down and wiggling fingers.
    4. Then inhale and sing (your choice of exercise or phrase).

LESSON ONE-B

Vocal Placement—The Floating Tone continued

CONCEPT:

TONE SHOULD BE EVEN AND STRONG, BUT NOT FORCED:

The tone should have a full, focused sound, not thin nor thin and spread out. The tone should be solid, full, supported, vibrant, resonant and energetic. In other words, it should have resonance and energy.

DEFINITION
- Focus the tone, refers to a narrowing of the cheeks as in an "oo" or a whistle, and supporting the tone so that it has intensity of sound.

EXPERIMENT
- To test for pushing, using your shoulders, arms and hands, push hard against a wall while singing. This will take the harsh energy away physically and thus you can tell if your are forcing the tone.
- Be sure to keep the cheeks narrow to maintain the focus. Be careful not to overdo this.

Exercise:
- For a bigger tone, or stronger, more even tone, try a "resistance" technique by placing hands against a stationary object like to a wall. Then on high notes, press firmly to keep from stretching.

EXERCISE:
- To help strengthen the tone, blow out strongly using the resistance of "SSSSSSSSSS" and feel pressure against the chest.

BRIGHT VOWEL MODIFICATION:

Narrowness of the pharynx combined with a lower larynx and nasal resonance will make a bright vowel richer.

EXERCISE:
Cheek Blowing Exercise. Keeping your mouth closed and holding your nose, "blow up" your cheeks. Keep the air pressure going against your cheeks and nose for approximately 8 seconds. Release breath. This exercise can be used to help with high tones in lesson or practice by stopping before a high tone, do the exercise and then immediately exhale followed by inhaling and singing the pitch.

APPROACHING A LOW TONE

When you are having problems starting on a low pitch, try working down lightly from a 5th above the note downward in diatonic pitches as in sol, fa, mi, re, do. Approach this gently and without dropping heavily on the tones. See Exercise #5 in Appendix.

CONCEPT:

Think of water skiing with your arms extended. Your goal is to stay up on the water and remain extended and energetic. Once you let down, you will go under the water. Now lower your arms and remain high and alert.

IF PLACEMENT OF TONE SOUNDS LIKE IT IS PRODUCED ON ONE SIDE

- Sometimes it may seem as if the tone is coming from one side of the face.
- Have the student open his/her mouth and check to see if the mouth or jaw is pulled to one side. Temporomandibular joint disorder or TMJ syndrome may cause this. This position may prevent the resonance from going up evenly into the facemask, but may pull the tone to one side as well. It can also cause a tension in the throat as the muscles will not be working evenly.

- Could also be caused by uneven posture due to one leg being longer than the other. A chiropractor could tell.
- Another cause could be from an obstruction in the sinuses. Often any of these problems need to be assessed by a physician.

EXERCISE:
- Lean over while singing "huNG". Let your head and neck relax, then <u>slowly</u> rise up (vertebrae by vertebrae) still singing "NG". Feel the vibrations move as you bend over, then try to keep the vibrations in that same spot as you straighten up. This exercise relaxes the back of the neck and relates to the voice box, which lies straight across from it.

CONCEPT:

Sometimes we have found keyboard players following the notes on a page up and down as on a keyboard or the musical staff; it may be very slightly and perhaps even only mentally. This image can cause an uneven tone quality. Imagine instead, a clothesline with the notes "hanging at different lengths" from the line with the line supporting the notes.

LESSON TWO

The Effect Of Speech Patterns
[This comes from a conversation with Eileen Davis]

SPEECH PATTERNS: The speaking voice can give clues to correcting the singing voice. The speaking voice can also positively influence the singing voice. For instance . . .

EXPERIMENT
- Speak using a guttural, throaty voice. Feel how low in the throat the vibration and sensations are. They might be described as a closed throat, with a very gravelly sound and pushed from the throat feeling.
- Then speak like a "British Lady" in a high, operatic speaking voice and feel where the sensations are. They might be described as open throated, high in the head, a free and easy feeling.

EXERCISE
- Imitate the British Lady's high voice with sentences like: *"Ah'd lahke to rahde Misses Ahastuhr's whaht peht hawrse."* [I'd like to ride Mrs. Astor's white pet horse]

YOUNG BOYS

As boys experience the vocal change as they approach puberty, be aware that they may try to "manufacture" a man's sound to overcome the embarrassment of the instability of their changing voice. More on this in Chapter 7, Lesson 3.

IN AMERICAN ENGLISH: the ends of spoken phrases or sentences inflect downward. This downward inflection carries over to singing making it a natural inclination to "drop" the sound lower in the throat, especially as the pitch goes lower and at the ends of phrases, or on an "AY" or "EE".

LESSON THREE

What Else Can Affect Tone Quality?

CHECK THE FOLLOWING WHEN WORKING TO CORRECT TONE QUALITY:

- Is breath support weak?
- Is vowel being molded correctly or with the proper modification?
- Is the vowel manipulated with the jaw, instead of lips and cheeks?
- Is there a "spreading" of the tone, instead of a roundness and narrowness?
- Is the jaw being "dropped" as opposed to the cranial lift? [See Chapter 1, Lesson 4]
- Is the throat tight?
- Is the larynx too high?

Lazy speech, slow tongue, and slurred articulation will cause two things: 1) the loss of breath and 2) voice placement going backward. By using a crisp articulation, the voice is brought forward and less breath is used.

Raising the eyebrows can affect a high tone by making it sound "stretched". Be sure to relax the eyebrows, especially when singing high.

Carrying a "heavy" tone upward can cause difficulties in hitting the tone on pitch. Be sure to lighten on the high tones. In a related way, on low notes, start with the space you'll need later for higher note in the phrase.

Anything overdone can be wrong. Vocal adjustments are almost always small adjustments!

In the low register, the teacher should listen for a certain amount of head resonance above the tone.

In the high register, notes with a bit of a low quality will have a natural vibrato.

CONCEPT:

Again, think of water skiing. In order to keep up on the water, one doesn't slump in posture. This will keep you feeling up and ready with all your muscles. This also enhances confidence.

CONCEPT:

When we refer to "spread" sound, we are referring to the sound created by lips too horizontal and mouth in too closed a position. The tongue should have a spread out look to it (again like "a" in the word "cat".)

PHRASE PRACTICE

Vowels can be modified with hints of other vowels. Practicing a song phrase by phrase on a single vowel can help the tone. If the sound is too dark, use an "a" (as in "cat") or "ay" (as in "say") or "ee" (as in "see"). If the sound is too bright, use "oh" (as in "hoe") or "oo" (as in "shoe"). Note that a teacher needs to listen to determine the quality of darkness or brightness of tone and decide the best vowel to use.

EXERCISE

To enhance chest resonance and depth, pound all over chest, like a gorilla. This relaxes chest muscle area and loosens tightness in the bronchial area.

LESSON FOUR

The Hard And Soft Palates

DEFINITION
- The hard palate is the roof of the mouth. See illustration in Chapter 3, Lesson 1.

CONCEPT:
Keeping the soft and hard palates lifted will help direct the sound to a higher place in the head. It keeps the sound from having a forced, pushed quality and helps to float the tone.

EXERCISE
- To strengthen the hard palate muscles, suck on something, like a collapsed straw, a piece of hard candy, etc.

EXERCISE
- Whisper "Kee, Kee, Kee" (rest, repeat)—quickly (as in 16th notes.) The "k" should be with a forward placement of the tongue.

DEFINITION
- The soft palate is the soft area at the uvula and behind it.

EXERCISE:
THIS EXERCISE COMES FROM THE OTOLARYNGOLOGY & VOCAL THERAPY DEPARTMENT OF THE OHIO STATE UNIVERSITY.

Use this exercise to strengthen the soft palate.
- Watch in a mirror and raise the uvula up and down 10 times, working up to fifty times in the following manner: lift 10 times, rest, lift 10 times and repeat until you've reached your goal number.

- Then, lift and hold for 10 seconds, relax for 10 seconds. Work up to 5 times.

CONCEPT:
A low soft palate can create a "swallowed" sound. The correction to this may be a combination of vowels, like "ee-oh-ee-oh" while keeping the same palate position and keeping both vowels in the same mold. Be careful that on an "OO" or "OH" the soft palate does not go too low.

CONCEPT:
The Pear Shaped Tone.

Imagine the stem of the pear as your tongue, the small round part the hard palate and mouth area and the large round part the soft palate and throat. When lifting the soft palate, be careful that the tongue stays forward and does not get the base of it pulled into a swallowed, back position.

EXERCISE:
Sigh on an octave top to bottom using a sigh-yawning like sound "Aw____". See Exercise #52 in Appendix.

EXERCISE:
See Exercise #35 in Appendix. "Giddy up" is sung with round, light and quick tones. This works to relax the tongue as well.

LESSON FIVE
The "Cover"

MISCONCEPTION:

- The cover is often a misunderstood term. The question arises as to what is being covered and what sound is the teacher asking for.

CONCEPT:

- The point of using the cover is to even out the range and keep the same quality of sound from register to register in the voice.
- Eleanor Steber said that the cover tone is breath hitting the hard palate in line with the eyes. It places the tone in the mask.
- Start with a very soft tone. The cover always starts with a soft volume and light tone approach.
- When singing softly, one cannot lighten the support. Keep the same intensity of sound. In other words, keep the same intensity of support in both loud and soft, just change the volume. The resonance of the facemask will indicate the intensity of the sound. Note that in the cover there is even a slight increase of energy.
- Prior to a top tone, lighten. To lighten means to approach the tone gently, but maintain support. Imagine a clarinet—in order to go softer in volume, the support must continue without pinching off the sound.

TO COVER A TONE

- Tilt the head slightly forward (like a marionette with the head string attached at the crown) to "throw" the tone high in the head behind the eyes and nose. Then when opening up the sound remain in the higher position. Be careful that you tilt the head slightly and do not tuck the chin, because that will cramp the space.

RULES OF THE COVER—from Eleanor Steber

- Cover before to a top tone
- Cover all descending scales
- Cover between the semitones (1/2 steps); in a slow, diatonic scales, cover the semi-tones.
- Descending pitches

The cover is used to make transitions easier, causing a smooth and seamless scale and range of notes. It "knits" the registers together so there's no change in the quality of sound. When jumping to another pitch higher, the cover helps prepare for an increased volume without pushing the sound.

When ascending, the cover allows a better approach to the swelling out of the volume. It keeps the vibration higher up in the head.

The cover stabilizes the control of the tone even in descending a scale. All this is in the effort to keep from "dropping" the scale notes. It keeps the note on pitch and keeps it from going flat.

Some of Eleanor Steber's remarks about the cover included:

- Cover should never be excessive or unnatural.
- Ends of some phrases should be covered.
- A tone preceding a climatic high tone should be covered then the high tone released open.
- In scales of slow tempo (as in a diatonic movement) cover the semi-tones.
- The higher register should be carried down over one, two or three notes of the adjacent register.
- Changing tones between registers should be light and covered and sung with care.

- In the scale, start with a soft smile on the low tone; in high D and E of scale those two covered then open up into the F. Descending cover the E and D as in up, at A you can softly smile again.
- The smile in cover should never be excessive or unnatural.

Teacher's additional ideas

CHAPTER FIVE

Legato and Staccato Articulation

LESSON ONE
Legato

DEFINITION: LEGATO refers to a smooth and unbroken flow of tones in a phrase.

CONCEPT:

Legato can be described like a string of pearls or it can be thought of as pulling taffy being careful that the taffy does not break.

WHAT AFFECTS A LEGATO SOUND

- Diction can affect legato. Clipping the ends of words especially with the consonants will destroy the legato line. [More about this in Chapter 6, Lesson 4]
- The tongue pulling, or moving in the back of the throat can cause an uneven, non-legato sound.
- Not using the cover
- Legato is dependent on tone quality.

CONCEPT:

One of the goals in singing is to have a smooth and even scale, bridging the gaps between registers. A trained ear of a teacher can pick up on this problem. [See Chapter 7, Lesson 2 about registers.]

EXERCISE: "Oh-Ay"
This exercise will allow the teacher to hear unevenness in tone, legato, placement. See Exercise #1 in Appendix.

CONCEPT:

One needs to keep the breath pressure even and never diminish. In other words "Keep blowing out!" Imagine a fountain. The water has to keep coming out at an even rate. When the pressure lets up, the water "dribbles" instead of springing forth.

CONCEPT:

Breath must flow forward through each phrase, like going over a mountain. You go over, not sliding back down the same side.

Recall Chapter 2, Lesson 4 in which the ball is being kept afloat on top of a stream of air. Or, imagine the space shuttle; the lift off takes lots of energy and then as it goes on the shuttle seems to float.

LESSON TWO

Staccato

DEFINITION: STACCATO refers to the separating one note from another. Detached. Opposite of legato.

CONCEPT:

Staccato notes are high in head with the tone at the same place as the legato notes. Be careful to approach them lightly and to not land heavily on the notes in a way that causes them to be flat and not focused.

CONCEPT:

The tongue may interfere in the production of a staccato. Tongue may try to cut off the air, which might indicate lack of breath support. It may tighten and bunch up.

CONCEPT:

Staccato is a bouncing feeling. Approach the staccato by thinking of a tire with an inner tube—your inner abs are the inner tube and are flexible, they "pump" the staccato. Your outer abs are the outer tire and provide support. Or, think of a mallet striking a xylophone. The muscles are mallet-like.

EXERCISE:
Pant like a dog, starting slowly and the gradually accelerate. These are the staccato muscles and muscle action.

CONCEPT:
QUALITIES OF A GOOD STACCATO:

- Clarity of tone
- Crispness—like all the muscles are working together in synchronization.
- Clean attack and release. Not a glottal attack. Muscles tighten-relax in rapid succession.
- Relaxed and natural

Teacher's additional ideas

CHAPTER SIX

Diction (in English)

LESSON ONE
The Lips, Vowels, Diphthongs

Do not tighten the jaw on the vowel "ee" and do not overly close the mouth. Practice the blending of these vowels using Exercise #2 in Appendix. Choose various vowel combinations like "ee-oo" "ay-oh" and "oh-ay". When going from a vowel, like "ee" to an vowel, like "oh", do not let the "oh" drop, or the upper lip pull downward.

CONCEPT:
THE EFFECT OF LIPS ON TONE:

Be sure not to tuck your chin and/or move upper lip over the upper teeth (resembling a turtle). Although this may seem to make the high notes easier, it takes away a fullness of sound and makes the tone seem shallow and too bright.

CONCEPT:

On an "oh" be sure to actively engage the cheek muscles in the formation of the vowel, but do not overdo. It helps to narrow the mouth when going into head voice, then relax to a little wider form in the high tones.

DIPHTHONGS:

EXAMPLE: "Ou" (as in ouch) or "ow" (as in now) = AH + oo

Be careful to maintain support and pitch for the 2nd sound in a diphthong. It is too easy to lower the inflection and support for the 2nd sound in the same way that we drop the ends of sentences in our speech with the sound falling into the throat and becoming a more guttural sound.

Closing the mouth too soon before the completion of the 2nd sound of the diphthong will cause a change in the tone.

OTHER DIPHTHONGS: All of the long vowels except "ee" are diphthongs as follows:
- Long "I" (as in lie) is a combination of AH with an ee ending
- Long "A" (as in say) is a combination of EH with an ee ending
- Long "O" (as in sew) is an OH with an oo ending
- "AH" (as in "father") is an AH with an ee ending.
- Long "U" (as in "use") will begin with ee and end in OO. Note that the main sound is the 2nd one in this instance.

Also included in diphthong sounds are:
Words like "our" which is AW with "oor" ending and "fire" which is FAW with an "er" ending. Most words ending with an "r" will be diphthongs because of the "er" sound.

CONCEPT:
"AH" SOUND:

"AH" can have one of 2 problems, it is either too bright sounding, or too low in the throat, making it sound dull.

The following exercise will help to make the correct "AH" sound:

EXERCISE: On a single note blend from "OH" to "AH" back to "OH" and again to "AH" and repeat. Try to keep the same high placement in the head. An "AH" should be modified with the vowel "OH".

CONCEPT:
VOCAL RESONANCE:

In every vowel, there should be a resonant focal point that keeps a similar resonance, focal point and timbre from the preceding vowels. The outcome is a well blended sound that keeps the continuity of the total voice.

In diction, please do not look as if you are chewing the words. Very little jaw movement is needed. It is more important to keep a similar focal point and blending of the vowels.

LESSON TWO

Consonants

CONCEPT:

When beginning a phrase, one should be sure that the consonant begins "on the exact pitch of the note" to prevent a sliding of the sound. If a consonant is not on the same level as the 1st note, then the rest of the phrase will be flat. Starting flat, that is under the pitch creates a heaviness that is difficult to correct once you are already in the phrase.

Notice if the tongue is starting in the correct position, that is touching the back and sides of the bottom teeth. Is it affecting the jaw and or the muscle under the chin? [Refer to Chapter 3, Lesson 1 under the heading "Tongue Tension" and notice the tongue structure in the illustration.] A tongue in the incorrect position will change the breath flow and placement. Keep the consonants light.

Look out for preparing the consonants too soon, which will destroy the legato line and affect the tone quality.

USE OF THE TONGUE FOR FORWARD CONSONANTS, ESPECIALLY "D" "L" "N" "T"

No jaw movement is involved with the production of "D" "L" "N" "T", only the tip of the tongue touching the back of the upper teeth. The lower jaw does not drop appreciably in these consonants. Think the phrase "Tip of the tongue, to the tip of the teeth."

EXERCISE:

Speak or sing on a single note: "Doh, noh, loh, noh, doh". The tongue touches the gum ridge back of the upper front teeth and there is no jaw movement.

An "L" is often formed too far back in the mouth: use only the tip of the tongue. The same problem occurs with the "K". With a "K" use only the forward part of the tongue.

CONCEPT:

Upon going to a high tone in the range, modify the consonant, so as not to over articulate it. A strongly articulated consonant can cause too much heaviness. For example: in the word "white", soften the "w". [Note that "w" is started with an "oo" sound, so do not use a tight "oo"]. Blow lightly with a more open mouth. Use more spacing all the way down the throat. Resonance needs to be a part of the equation.

Consonants held too long can bog down the tempo of a piece. Consonants also drag down the vocal placement when they are held too long. The word "what" is especially troublesome as commonly spoken. It often takes too much time on the "wh" sound. An exception is when called for by the composer or for an effect that is desired by a conductor or performer, often a more pronounced "m" or "n". Too long on consonants can also use up the breath.

Avoid the common mistake of pronouncing the word "you" preceded by an ending "t" as in "got you" as "chew".

LESSON THREE

Modifying The Vowel

CONCEPT:

- As the pitch goes higher, modify the vowel toward "uh". Do not take the pure vowel up high.
- As the pitch goes into the low range, there is a modification toward more rounding of the lips and a slight closing of the mouth.
- One wrong vowel modification or placement affects all others after it.
- "EE" and "AY" need space in the back of the throat. More about that below.

CONCEPT:

It often helps to overdo another sound in an exercise to let the residual of that sound temper the problem with the tone of the vowel. For instance a very bright Ī (as in "night") when the "i" would be pronounced almost with an Ī sound use the following exercise:

EXERCISE:
[Spoken in an over exaggerated way.] "YAW, YAW, YAW, YAW, YAW, YAW, YAW____."

When changing vowels to "OH" or "OO" lips should be rounded and move forward, not down. Lips just can't be up, but should move forward.

A clenched jaw can cause a change in focus and tone quality that is not desirable. To correct this, try singing "OH" then blend to "EE" with very little change so as to keep the space. "AY" may cause the same problem. Follow the same cure only use "OH" to "AY".

"Ay" and "Ee" can be modified according to pitch just using more space as one goes higher. Likewise going high to low, there will be a point where the mouth needs to start closing so it can keep the tone focused. For a soprano these changes begin around the "c" above "Middle C"

In lower registers on "EE" and "AY", more spacing in the back will help keep the sound from being too bright.

A poorly pronounced vowel can be tempered by blending it with another vowel. Like "ee" tempered with "oo" or "oh" as in the word "need". We often tell out students to put a little more "oo" in the "ee" sound. Having done the earlier exercises of the quick change between "oo" and "ee", they seem to understand this terminology. Likewise, one can do this with any vowel, depending on the desired outcome. "Aw" may sound too dark, and can be tempered with "ee" or "ay" or "a". "Ah" may sound too bright, and can be tempered with "oo" or "oh" and so forth.

The English language can come with built in problems depending on the local dialect. We suggest using Italian as the first foreign language because it is more consistent in its pure vowel sounds.

Properly pronounced vowels will help to bring the voice to a more forward and higher place in the head.

EXPERIMENT:
Repeat quickly "oh-ay-oh-ay-oh-ay-oh-ay" then say, "Away we go!!" If done with enthusiasm there should be a noticeable sound of the speaking voice being much higher in the head than before.

LESSON FOUR

The Rules Of Diction

First Rule:

When a consonant ending one word or syllable is followed by another consonant, place the 1st consonant on the 2nd one.
- For example:
  The phrase "time tumbles" becomes "Tah__mtuh___mbluh__ls." Hold the vowel as long as possible. The "mt" is one unit, don't think about "m" and don't accent the "m", just use a little sound, unaccented.

  Closing on the 1st consonant when going to a high note from a low one will destroy the high tone, making it too difficult. It makes the low note too heavy to be prepared for the high one.

Second Rule:

Get rid of consonants quickly.
- For example:
  The phrase "Young and" becomes "Yuh__(ng)a_____nd"

Third Rule:

With the exception of singing the extreme high notes of the range, ending percussive consonants <u>must</u> be articulated, but <u>not prolonged.</u> The breath needs to continue to flow through the consonant.

Fourth Rule:

A consonant followed by a consonant, place a quickly articulated "uh" to the first consonant.
- For example:
A consonant followed by the <u>same consonant</u>, both of which need to be articulated for clarity of the meaning of the word, place a very light and quick "uh" between them as in "need Diane" becomes "nee__(duh)Di__ane."

- Another example:
A consonant followed by a <u>different consonant</u> as in "Time goes" becomes "Tah__m(uh)goh___z"

- A third example:
A <u>consonant at the end of a phrase</u> place a quickly articulated "uh" attached to it as in "ate" becomes "lay____t(uh)." This "uh" sound is not dropped pitch-wise, but supported with the breath and continued on the same mental line as the preceding "lay" sound.

Teacher's additional ideas

CHAPTER SEVEN

*Registers and classifying the voice,
working with children
and the male voice*

LESSON ONE
Chest, Middle, Passáge, Head, Whistle, Falsetto

VOCAL REGISTERS

DEFINITION:
Different sections of the scale of the voice are characterized by a change in quality. We call these sections vocal registers.

The singer needs to learn to bridge from one to another smoothly and have no sound of a "break" in the voice. The lower registers need to blend with the head voice. When going to the higher registers, one needs to use the cover, lighten and use good support. More information of this is in Lesson 2 of this chapter.

CHEST VOICE

DEFINITION:
The lowest tones of the range. In the soprano this may extend to the A below Middle C.

The tendency is to be too heavy and push low in the throat and chest area.

CONCEPT:

When singing in low chest voice, focus tones forward toward the front teeth and hitting the hard palate. Sing on the breath with no tension or heaviness on the vocal mechanism.

MIDDLE VOICE:

DEFINITION:
The middle of the range. In the soprano these notes are generally D above Middle C up to Treble C or D; upper middle goes on up to F or F#. The area of the upper middle voice is often referred to as the "passáge". More on that further on in this lesson.

HEAD VOICE:

DEFINITION:
The head voice is the upper range and will feel high in the head. In the soprano it begins around High G and goes to the High C. Going into upper head register there will be a slight spreading of the lips.

WHISTLE:

DEFINITION:
The upper most part of the range. In the soprano, any notes above High C. There is a distinct narrowing of the sound in these extremely high notes.

FALSETTO:

DEFINITION:
In the male voice this defines the range that begins to have a more feminine timbre to it.

OLDER VOICES

Older voices may change due to hormonal changes or lack of muscle tone or both. Muscle tone can be improved with exercise, both physical and vocal.

CONCEPT:
PRINCIPLES OF THE PASSÁGE

DEFINITION: Passáge is French for passage. In female voices the passáge is from one register to another. The passáge is a graduation of sound quality. For instance, for a soprano, the notes of treble D, E, and F are the passáge notes between middle and head voice.

Where the passáge areas lie is a factor in classifying a voice. [See Chapter 7, Lesson 4 about if and when to classify a voice] In the female voice, the crucial point is F/F# before the pure head voice of "G". If the change is lower, the classification may be lower.

In the passáge there needs to be a lightening of the voice so there's not a "break" in the sound. In this case we cover the voice between ½ tones. And remember, previous to a top tone, one should cover and lighten.

More about voice classification in Chapter 7, Lesson 3.

LESSON TWO

Bridging The Gap Between Registers

DEFINITION: Bridging the gap refers to smoothing out the range with the objective of having no noticeable change in tone quality when singing a scale, top to bottom. This should be a blending of tones from one tone to the next one.

CONCEPT:

- A Rule of Thumb for register changing: Take a register down 3 notes into the next.
- Going up, do not spread the lips side to side although the higher pitches will take more space. Be sure the jaw is relaxed. Use the cranial lift. Say with feeling, 'OUCH' 3 times, keeping the face mask resonance.
- For women, high A, B & C may spread a little for a mushroom effect. Narrowness is really important through the passáge.
- Re-support and lighten over ½ tones, up or down.
- Keep the support even as you descend to lower notes.
- Practice the tongue exercises as the tongue tends to cause problems between registers.
- Review "the cover".

CONCEPT:
SINGING HIGHER TO LOWER

- When working on bridging the gaps between registers, use exercises that begin high and go low.
- Keep the low support strong as you descend the notes.
- Keep the resonance high in the head. Keep the uvula raised up.

- Often around 2nd space treble A, one has a tendency to drop the tone and the support just at the moment when the support needs to be strengthened. The danger is that once the tone and support has dropped, it is difficult to turn that around to go back up higher. The remedy is to work at re-supporting the tones on the way down. By building the muscle tone of the breathing muscles this support will occur more naturally. Another remedy to avert tension in the re-support is to lean against or push against a wall while practicing.

EXPERIMENT:
Think going up as you sing going down. It may help to use your hand and arm, palm upward and gesture raising the arm and hand up as you sing the descending pitches. This can help keep the tone on the higher level, avoiding a drop in posture and in pitch.

CONCEPT:
SINGING LOWER TO HIGHER

- Keep all notes from the position of the higher note. To find that higher position, to sing higher note and gently move downward to the lower tone and then go back up to the higher tone without breathing or stopping. Then repeat, but this time stop to breathe, begin as you ended on the low note and go back up to the high note.
- Don't forget "the cover".
- Check tongue position. Is it forward and relaxed, or tightly bunched up, "U" shaped or pulled back?
- Keep the larynx in the low position.

EXPERIMENT:
This experiment should be done only after the singer understands the correct way to sing the chest register. It should not be overdone. The purpose of the experiment is to help lower the larynx. In a low, nasal chest-voice sing "Hee" for 4-6 counts creating a resistance in the chest. This should strengthen the muscles that control the larynx as well as relax the chest muscles.

The teacher looks and listens for . . .
- Position of the larynx; it should be low.

- The shape of the mouth. Is it rounded and narrowed with the "OH" shape or incorrectly spread side to side or is the upper lip drawn down?
- Where is the tongue; it should be very far forward. It should remain still and relaxed.
- Is the sound smooth and effortless, or does it sound gulping or glottal or some other kind of non-musical sound?

LESSON THREE

If And When A Voice Can/Should Be Classified, Teaching Children And Working With The Male Voice

CLASSIFYING THE VOICE—THE CASE AGAINST
In our opinion, teachers should not classify a voice until the voice is free of obstructions and singing properly AND of age vocally speaking. Too many times a voice is classified early on as one thing, and then the student allows herself/himself to be stereotyped in this classification and does not allow herself to develop her full voice. The case we have often faced is a girl who is classified as an alto, may be someone who has a good sense of pitch and can hold on to the lower part against a strong higher part. She may actually be a soprano, but the classification strongly influences her to think of herself only in terms of being an alto. A comfortable tessitura is more important. Too high can fatigue the vocal mechanism. Too low can push on the vocal cords. In either case the voice can be damaged.

CONCEPT:
THE "MANUFACTURED" VOICE

Sometimes a singer will try to convince others that the voice is higher or lower than it actually is. To recognize this manufactured voice listen for the following:
- When the voice lays too high, there will be an edge and dullness of tone. *(example here)*
- When the voice lies too low, the sound will be dark and overdone.

CONCEPT:
STUDENT RELUCTANCE:

A student may be reluctant to change. Especially in exploring the head register. Use the "sigh" exercise on an "OO" or "KOO" See Exercise #52 in Appendix. Try imitating the up and down whine of a siren.

CONCEPT:
HOW LEARNING PROPER TECHNIQUE CAN AFFECT THE RANGE:

A tessitura can change as the learning process happens—<u>the tone</u> comes <u>from</u> the energy, <u>not the energy</u> from the tone. So, you may need to experiment with various ranges and not stay "set". Breathing, relaxation, breath energy being developed will certainly help a voice with a naturally high tessitura.

CORE OF THE VOICE

DEFINITION: The individual quality that everyone has. The sound that distinguishes one individual voice from another.
- Using the vocal mechanism properly will enhance the unique quality and will affect the vibrato.
- Once the core of the voice is found, classification will be easier and more correct.

TEACHING A CHILD

- <u>Never</u> brand a child with a classification.
- When working with children, do not work too long in one session.
- Keep the voice light. Discourage loudness, as loudness will place too much pressure on the vocal cords.
- Do work on matching pitches. Check out the Kodaly teaching method.
- Children should learn to listen critically and we need to be a good model.

A note about children and singing
- Many people are told from an early age that they can't sing. This may be because different children learn to match pitches at different

times. Exposure to singing and to music as well as being encouraged to sing will go a long way toward giving the child self-confidence and courage to try singing.
- Sometimes a child believes that if he/she does not sound as good as their parent (one who perhaps is an accomplished singer), that they can never learn to be as good and they constantly compare themselves to their parent or perhaps a sibling.
- In working with children be sure to keep the voice light and natural. The following are hints for working with children:
  o Hum or buzz in nose, lightly
  o Exercise:
      On a descending major chord in the mid-range, sing the words "I love ice cream" see Exercise #53 in Appendix.
  o Keep the music easy; consider rhythm, range and intervals. In the beginning minor 3rds and diatonic 2nds are easiest. For youngest children a very short range is most appropriate like the song "Rain, rain, go away".
  o Parental co-operation is essential. Parents need to reinforce the teacher's approach and not insist that the child sing "louder" or sing songs that are not appropriate to the child's ability or age.
  o Children can learn correct breathing in a modified way by not raising shoulders on intake of breath; careful not to pull in breath; relaxation on intake as in blow out all air, then just relax and let the air come in.
  o As for posture, imagining being a marionette with a string attached to the top of the head and being lifted up by the puppeteer is one visual way to get at proper posture. A fun exercise is to go limp, then let the puppeteer raise the string, and then go limp again. A game of "mother may I" or "Simon Says" can be made out of this and out of any of the posture and relaxing routines we've described in earlier chapters.

WORKING WITH THE MALE VOICE

- When the voice is changing, work on posture, breathing, vowel mold and blend in a very small range until the range extends both up and down.
- The larynx should be low. If problems continue with it being too high, try pounding the chest all over, ape-like, to loosen the chest

muscles. You may combine this with the low "hee" as described earlier and as follows: In a low, nasal chest-voice sing "hee" for 4-6 counts creating a resistance in the chest. This exercise can also be used in female singers who also may have a larynx that is too high.
- In the tenor "timbre", the top tones should not be forced; this can be corrected with floating lightness as described in Chapter 4 on tone quality. There is head resonance in the male voice but not a head voice register. Head resonance is <u>not</u> falsetto, which is a more feminine sound.
- Some work from the falsetto blending downward may help locate the upper tones. This is a discovery phase of learning and not to be used after the upper tones are developed.
- Again, the cover will work to bring about a good approach to high tones.
- Look for posture problems—Chest out, shoulders back (military style) would be wrong.
- Irish tenor is a good example of the light, beautiful approach to high tones.
- Working with the bass range, imagine an elevator gliding smoothly downward, not going "ker-plunk." Avoid using a manufactured tone.

CHAPTER EIGHT

The Performance

LESSON ONE

Performance Readiness

On the day of the performance, be well rested and avoid strenuous exercise, which will cause fatigue.

Mentally prepare your energy <u>before</u> you go out on stage.

Use warm-up exercises to get the voice moving; use your favorites. You might include 5-note scales on "Ma" or "Mi" or other vowels; 1 octave arpeggios legato and/or staccato; humming—"Silent Night" is a good tune for range, skips, up and down.

EXERCISE:
- When a performance is going to need a bit of energy, try singing while running across a room. This gives a feeling of resistance.

CONCEPT:
PREPARE A PERFORMING FRAME OF MIND

- Create the thought of energy, a feeling of a light mood. Keep bright, smiling eyes. You must put away any sadness, tiredness, or depressing thoughts <u>before</u> you are on stage. Walk on stage (or even into your lesson) ready to sing with spirit and energy. Even if it is a sad song, keep the lift and energy, but of course remember it <u>is</u> a sad song. This is much like creating a character in acting.
- Blow out all your air, relax and allow the air to come in. Hold it as long as possible, and then release the air. This helps relax tension and begin the energy building process.
- Warm up muscles with stretches and perhaps brief light exercises, like the ones in Chapter 1, Lesson 3.

- **Be secure in the words and music of the repertoire to be performed.** Amateurs especially should practice with the accompanist more than once if possible, until the "bugs" are worked out and they feel comfortable as a team.

STAGE PRESENCE

- When performing, gaze above the tops of the heads of the audience, looking toward the rear of the room.
- Try to use your nervousness as a tool in producing energy and that special "zing" to an animated performance. Everyone get nervous, but when used in your favor, it can be a positive thing. We have had students who actually sing better in performance than in rehearsals because of the energy generated by nerves.
- Don't allow negative thoughts or they will become a self-fulfilling prophecy.
- In a recital type setting, be sure to take a moment before each song to think, breathe and prepare your mood and approach.

LESSON TWO

The Physical Experience

CONCEPTS:

- The whole body sings.
- Toning is the result of gradually building up any muscle or muscle group. Toning gives one a sense of readiness.
- Physical Stamina needs to be built gradually over a long periods of standing while singing. Building up of the vocal mechanism over time and consistent practice will help the voice sound stronger. Be careful not to over do it by trying to speed up the time factor. It will take whatever time it takes and we have to be satisfied with slow and steady progress.

PHYSICAL CAUSES OF VOCAL PROBLEMS:

- Phlegm and mucous are nature's way of soothing irritation. Whatever you are doing incorrectly may be one cause.
- Try to keep the throat from becoming dry and raw from irritation. Try talking with the voice "up"—not a higher pitch, but a higher placement; striking the hard palate.
- Also check the posture of the voice. Where is the larynx? Is the body in alignment?
- Over exercise will tear muscles down; over singing without proper conditioning could lead to vocal damage also.
- Be sure to drink plenty of fluids to keep the voice lubricated.

CONCEPT:

- Core body exercise, like pilates, can help develop the breath supporting muscles.

CAUTION CONCERNING PHYSICAL EXERCISE:

- Try to avoid anything that causes grunting, glottal stroke, neck tension or throat tension.
- Watch out for compensating for being out of shape, by using the neck, throat or tongue.
- Upon exertion, blow out with an open throat and relaxed tongue. Avoid throat tensions.
- Strenuous exercise on the day of a performance could cause a lack of energy due to the physical exertion. Light and easy warm up exercises can help get the body ready to perform.
- Just sing! Once the muscles used for singing are toned and strong, then you don't have to think so much about support, but instead come at the performance from an energy standpoint. Feel energetic; again, nerves can actually help build the energy.
- You may wish to use the exercise described in Chapter 4, lesson 1 to release the false vocal cords.
- Use your energy for "full body singing"!! Full body singing is using every inch of your being to produce the most vibrant sound and presence that you can.
- The best kind of exercise does not exert pressure on the neck and throat. Good exercises include swimming, yoga, tai chi, etc.
- Wrong breathing can be caused by sports that require a lot of running like tennis. One gets too used to breathing high up and shallow.

LESSON THREE

Food, Drink And Other Things That May Help Or Hurt The Voice

POSSIBLE GOOD AND BAD FOOD OR DRINK THAT AFFECT THE VOICE:

- Good: warm drinks, 1 Tab. lemon juice may help to clear the throat; gargle with salt water also relieves sore throat.
- Bad: orange juice, milk, ice cream, other dairy products may coat the throat and interfere with vocal production. Also, avoid eating a large meal before a performance, as it can inhibit a full breath.
- Note: There are many stories about what is good and bad, but in the end you really have to go on your own experience. It is as unique as each individual.

WHEN TO REST THE VOICE

- Under a doctor's orders
- When there is congestion or swelling of the vocal cords.
- When you feel like you've gone long enough and your vocal mechanism is tired.

PRACTICE TIME

- In the beginning, short practice times will help to start strengthening the vocal mechanism. Sing daily practicing 15 minutes and gradually increase the time as your voice grows stronger.
- Quit when the voice or body feels tired.
- **Daily practice** is necessary in order to build the muscles used in singing.

- When you are doing mundane, thoughtless work you can practice the engagement and release of the breathing muscles, the posture routine, the relaxing routine, or concentrating on one piece of one of the topics we've presented in this book.
- After an illness, work back slowly. Be aware of your own body signals.

ACID REFLUX DISEASE

- Needs to be diagnosed by otolaryngologist.
- Can cause problems for the singer and vocal cord damage.

ASTHMA

- Can have an impact on a singer, especially in the matter of breathing.
- Have this diagnosed.
- Follow recommended treatment
- Be aware of your body and breath.
- Sometimes hot caffeinated drinks help.

Teacher's additional ideas

CHAPTER NINE

Trilling

LESSON ONE

The Trill

Eleanor Steber maintained "The trill is the guardian angel of the voice for keeping it young and flexible."

It is best to understand the "cover" before studying trills and flexibility. See Chapter 4, Lesson 5.

CONCEPT:

Trilling is not yodeling. The sound stays in the head and uses the cover position—whereas yodeling is distinct change of register.

Start with the upper note when you are first learning to trill. The object is to sing in the position of the upper note using the cover for the lower one.

In practice, accent the top note to keep it high and in the upper placement. It should never "drop" to the lower note.

EXERCISE: Start slowly ||: cover—open :|| gradually faster. At fast speed, keep in the cover position. Keep it light and accurate. Practice trills on ½-steps; whole steps and 1 ½ steps (a minor 3rd). See Exercises # 56 & #57 in Appendix.

Teacher listens for: intonation; distinct pitches, but blended; high placement.

There are other advanced techniques, but we are not going to describe them in this book of fundamental singing.

Teacher's additional ideas

APPENDIX

Notes From Lessons With Eleanor Steber

The following are notes taken from lessons with Eleanor.

A. The breath (tone) hitting hard palate will set up vibrations within the resonant chambers in line with the place where the tones strike the hard palate.
B. The quality of tone is determined by the place where the breath hits the hard palate and the resonant chambers so activated. The position of head governs the direction of air stream.
C. Ever so slight incline of head accomplishes this. The chest, pharynx and nasal cavities act as resonators.

This method employs the careful and systematic use of the cover tone and the cross of the voice.

Cover tone {<u>never, never</u> excessive or unnatural.} The cover tone is breath hitting the hard palate in line with the eyes. Lightening of tone and use cover support with ever so slightly incline of head.

Systematic use of
1. Breath pressure
2. Smile and round position
3. Normal and cover tone.

Rules for cover tone, never in excess or unnatural
1. Descending scales
2. Pitches descending
3. Ascending in intervals of 3rds or more, attack cover and then less covered.

4. End of some phrases
5. Tone preceding climatic high tone must be covered high tone released open.
6. In rapid scales, you have systematic use of normal & cover tone with graded breath flow and cross of the voice.
7. Scales of slow tempo as in a diatonic scale cover semitones.

More Notes Taken From Lessons With Eleanor.

1. The cover tone is breath hitting the hard palate in line with the eyes. It places the tone in the mask.
2. "Montare il Fiato" is "Mounting of the breath"; lift a little
3. Cover all descending scales and any pitches descending. Ascending skips of 3rds or more approach with lightness, attack with the cover then lessen the cover.
4. Ends of phrases—cover
5. A tone preceding a climatic high tone must be covered; the high tone is released open.
6. In rapid scales, you have a systematic use of normal and covered tones. In that you use the cross of the voice of a smile and rounding.
7. Keep the rib cage expanded at all times.

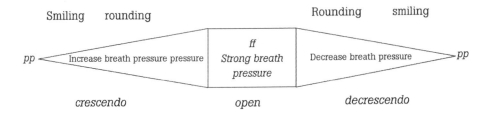

8. Messa de voce: the creascendo-dimenuendo [*pp* to *ff* to *pp*] is done with no unevenness of tone quality or tone placement. It must remain steady not letting it drop or forcing it up.
9. Breath in singing must be governed by the length of the phrases. Do not take full capacity for short phrases, there is no need to.
10. Eliminate all tension whether physical or psychological.

11. Do not force low voice up. Carry high voice down; only carry upper register down 3 semi-tones into the next register. The change between registers must be covered and light (of the adjacent tones)
12. Do not let the breath strike in the throat before it strikes the hard palate—causes flatness
13. Matter of proportion rather than volume. Molding of a phrase so that climax is achieved in the volume of scale capable of the singer. Never sacrifice beauty of tone for volume. Light tones correctly placed have quality, vitality and elasticity and flexibility.
14. Mr. Whitney: The quality of tone is determined by the place where the breath hits the hard palate and the resonance chamber so activated. The position of the head governs the direction of air stream. The ever so slight incline of head accomplishes this.

Eleanor Steber and Ruth Manahan

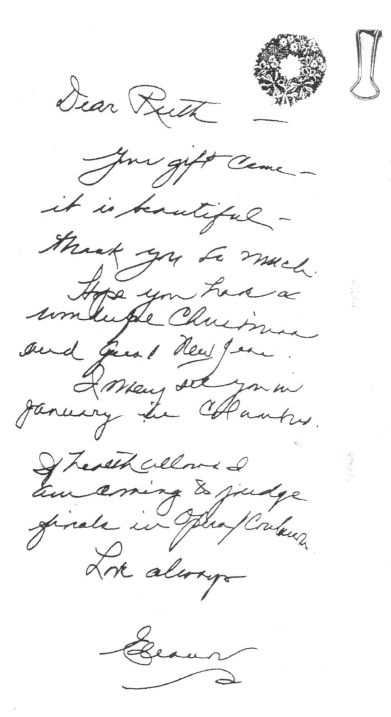

Note to Ruth Manahan from Eleanor Steber

UPON LOSING 100 POUNDS AND ITS EFFECT ON MY SINGING

This is my experience. It may not apply to everyone, but it could also explain some problems to someone else who may identify with my experience. I lost my weight from a gastric bypass procedure which was done laparoscopically with 5 abdominal incisions.

When I weighted 100 pounds more, my breath was shallow and labored. To relax and let go to breathe was not as easy as it sounds. I would drop the lower abdominal muscles and then had a difficult time repositioning them in a way that would support the sound. My knees and legs could hardly handle a 30 minute lesson of standing and I over compensated in my posture by leaning backwards to hold up my heavy stomach. I was exhausted just walking into the studio from my car.

Upon losing the weight, I definitely have more energy. I have more space for breath and my posture is easier to align properly. My abdominal muscles are still not toned to my satisfaction, but the weight loss has only been in the last 19 months at this writing. I'm working on my breathing using swimming and the exercises in the breathing chapter of this book as well as using an exercise ball for basic core muscle building. I am checking my posture alignment and making corrections using the Wii® fit program. I am building my stamina slowly but am determined to extend the time that I can stand without leaning on something or sitting down to rest.

I believe that we owe it to ourselves to find those things which enhance our physical being which in turn will improve our physical fitness for singing. Singing is physical as well as mental, and whatever we can to do to ready ourselves physically and/or mentally will affect our singing for the better.

Marise

VOCAL EXERCISES Ruth's use in book 2011 Feb 1

VOCAL EXERCISES
what they emphasize and how to use them.

VOCAL EXERCISES Ruth's use in book 2011 Feb 2

VOCAL EXERCISES Ruth's use in book 2011 Feb 5

VOCAL EXERCISES Ruth's use in book 2011 Feb 6

Printed in Great Britain
by Amazon.co.uk, Ltd.,
Marston Gate.